D0765664

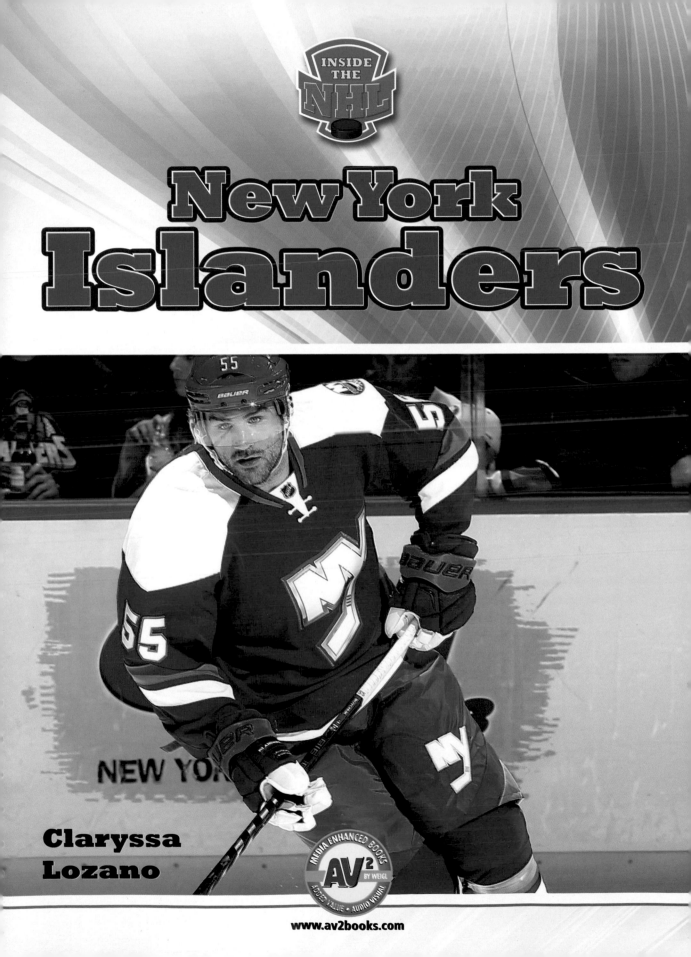

Inside the NHL

New York Islanders

Claryssa Lozano

AV² BY WEIGL
MEDIA ENHANCED BOOKS
ADDED VALUE • AUDIO VISUAL

www.av2books.com

MEDIA ENHANCED BOOKS
AV²
BY WEIGL™
ADDED VALUE • AUDIO VISUAL

AV² provides enriched content that supplements and complements this book. Weigl's AV² books strive to create inspired learning and engage young minds in a total learning experience.

Your AV² Media Enhanced books come alive with...

Audio
Listen to sections of the book read aloud.

Key Words
Study vocabulary, and complete a matching word activity.

Video
Watch informative video clips.

Quizzes
Test your knowledge.

Embedded Weblinks
Gain additional information for research.

Slide Show
View images and captions, and prepare a presentation.

Try This!
Complete activities and hands-on experiments.

... and much, much more!

Go to www.av2books.com, and enter this book's unique code.

BOOK CODE

Q636234

AV² by Weigl brings you media enhanced books that support active learning.

Published by AV² by Weigl
350 5th Avenue, 59th Floor
New York, NY 10118
Websites: www.av2books.com   www.weigl.com

Library of Congress Control Number: 2014951979

ISBN 978-1-4896-3161-9 (hardcover)
ISBN 978-1-4896-3162-6 (single-user eBook)
ISBN 978-1-4896-3163-3 (multi-user eBook)

Printed in the United States of America in Brainerd, Minnesota
1 2 3 4 5 6 7 8 9 0 19 18 17 16 15

032015
WEP050315

Senior Editor Heather Kissock
Art Director Terry Paulhus

Photo Credits
Every reasonable effort has been made to trace ownership and to obtain permission to reprint copyright material. The publishers would be pleased to have any errors or omissions brought to their attention so that they may be corrected in subsequent printings.

Weigl acknowledges Getty Images and iStock as its primary image suppliers for this title.

INSIDE THE NHL

New York Islanders

CONTENTS

Introduction

In 1972, the Islanders, or Isles, began playing in a state that had already hosted a hockey team for 46 years. New York was the home of the Rangers. Three-time division and Stanley Cup champions, the Rangers had already established themselves as a staple in New York sports. When the Islanders entered the scene, a rivalry was born, immediately making hockey much more interesting and exciting for New York residents.

Current captain John Tavares joined the Islanders in 2009.

The Islanders took their first steps to create a true rivalry during the 1974–1975 season. The Isles reached the **playoffs** for the first time that year, and they defeated the Rangers in the first round. From that point on, the teams have been on a seesaw, with each **franchise** winning four Stanley Cups. Today, the rivalry has cooled off a bit, but the Islanders came back for the 2014–2015 season with a renewed energy as they looked to give New York hockey fans another exciting run for the Cup.

The Isles last won the Stanley Cup in 1983. Though they reached the final in 1984, they lost to the Edmonton Oilers.

New York
ISLANDERS

Arena Barclays Center

Division Metropolitan

Head Coach Jack Capuano

Location Long Island, New York

NHL Stanley Cup Titles 1980, 1981, 1982, 1983

Nickname The Isles

8
Hall of Fame Players

6
Conference Championships

6
Division Championships

22
Playoff Appearances

History

8

former Islanders have been inducted into the NHL Hall of Fame.

Former captain Clark Gillies, sporting the signature Islanders beard, is one of six players to win the Stanley Cup four times with the Islanders.

With word that the World Hockey League (WHL) wanted to place a team in the Nassau Veterans Memorial Coliseum, the National Hockey League (NHL) was pressured to expand and bring another team to New York. In December 1971, 19 investors came together to purchase an NHL franchise that would call Long Island home. The group paid $6 million for the Islanders as well as a $4 million **territorial fee** to the New York Rangers.

Al Arbour became the Isles' coach in their second season, and although they finished last in their division for a second straight year, things were about to change. In year three, the Islanders reached the playoffs. The Islanders had become a powerful force in the NHL in a very short time. Soon, April, May, and June meant playoff time in Long Island as the Islanders qualified for the postseason 14 times in a row. It was during this remarkable playoff run that the team won four straight Stanley Cups, from 1980 to 1983. This is one of the greatest winning streaks in the history of the NHL.

Before signing on as the Islanders' coach, Al Arbour had played for the Detroit Red Wings, the Chicago Blackhawks, the Toronto Maple Leafs, and the St. Louis Blues.

The Arena

SMITH 31

NYSTROM 23

BOSSY 22

TROTTIER 19

GILLIES 9

POTVIN 5

1500

"The Architect"

Retired numbers are proudly hung from the rafters at the Coliseum.

Nassau Veterans Memorial Coliseum opened in 1972 and hosted its first hockey game on October 7. Though the Islanders lost that first game, the local fans remained enthused. They continued to fill the seats at the Coliseum night in and night out.

The Coliseum is currently the second-oldest arena in active use by an NHL team. As the arena became outdated and obsolete, some Islanders owners worked to try to replace it. Originally built to hold 15,000 spectators, the arena seating was expanded and can now hold 18,000 guests.

In 2011, extensive improvements were finally approved for the home of four Stanley Cup titles. The $229 million project will completely re-create the arena and add a shopping plaza and restaurants. Despite this, the Coliseum will no longer house the Islanders after the 2014–2015 season. Instead, the team will move to the Barclays Center in Brooklyn, New York.

Singer Beyoncé performed in Barclays Center in December 2013.

Where They Play

NHL WESTERN CONFERENCE

PACIFIC DIVISION

1 Anaheim Ducks
2 Arizona Coyotes
3 Calgary Flames
4 Edmonton Oilers

5 Los Angeles Kings
6 San Jose Sharks
7 Vancouver Canucks

CENTRAL DIVISION

8 Chicago Blackhawks
9 Colorado Avalanche
10 Dallas Stars
11 Minnesota Wild

12 Nashville Predators
13 St. Louis Blues
14 Winnipeg Jets

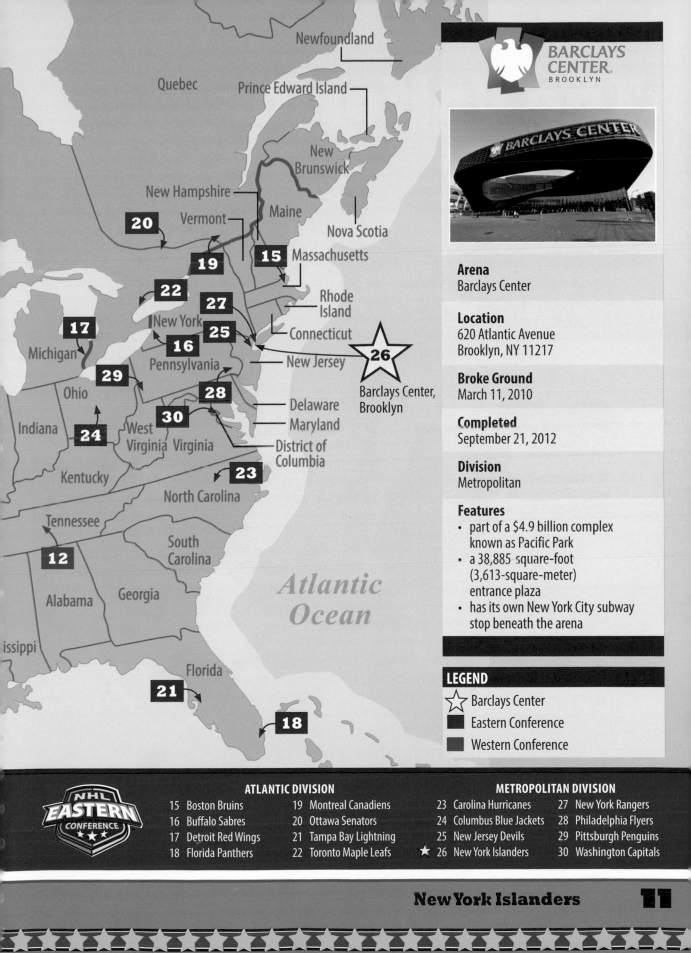

Map Labels

Newfoundland

Quebec

Prince Edward Island

New Brunswick

New Hampshire

Vermont

Maine

Nova Scotia

Massachusetts

Rhode Island

Connecticut

New York

New Jersey

Pennsylvania

Michigan

Ohio

Indiana

West Virginia

Virginia

Delaware

Maryland

District of Columbia

Kentucky

North Carolina

Tennessee

South Carolina

Alabama

Georgia

Mississippi

Florida

Atlantic Ocean

Barclays Center, Brooklyn

Arena
Barclays Center

Location
620 Atlantic Avenue
Brooklyn, NY 11217

Broke Ground
March 11, 2010

Completed
September 21, 2012

Division
Metropolitan

Features
- part of a $4.9 billion complex known as Pacific Park
- a 38,885 square-foot (3,613-square-meter) entrance plaza
- has its own New York City subway stop beneath the arena

LEGEND

☆ Barclays Center

■ Eastern Conference

■ Western Conference

NHL EASTERN CONFERENCE

ATLANTIC DIVISION

15 Boston Bruins
16 Buffalo Sabres
17 Detroit Red Wings
18 Florida Panthers
19 Montreal Canadiens
20 Ottawa Senators
21 Tampa Bay Lightning
22 Toronto Maple Leafs

METROPOLITAN DIVISION

23 Carolina Hurricanes
24 Columbus Blue Jackets
25 New Jersey Devils
★ 26 New York Islanders
27 New York Rangers
28 Philadelphia Flyers
29 Pittsburgh Penguins
30 Washington Capitals

The Uniforms

The Islanders have 7 retired jersey numbers.

With the exception of their 1995–1997 jerseys, the New York Islanders have used the same iconic design on their gear in every season they have played. The design displays the New York abbreviation with a hockey stick cleverly attached to the "Y" and has an image of Long Island in the background.

Since the team's very first season, the Islanders' uniforms have featured three main colors, blue, orange, and white. For 13 years, the team's jerseys remained the same with only minor variations. In 1995, the team introduced a new fisherman **logo** and added stripes of aqua to its uniform. The new logo was not popular and only lasted for two seasons.

HOME

The Islanders then replaced their bright blue and orange with a dull orange and navy blue. In 2008, however, they brought back their iconic bright blue, first as an alternate jersey, and eventually again as their primary home jersey. In 2011, the team added a black alternate jersey.

AWAY

In early 2014, the Islanders played at famous Yankee Stadium wearing a new alternate jersey. The jersey showcased an eye-catching NY logo that was sleek and modern.

Helmets and Face Masks

HELMET VISORS were made mandatory for new players during the 2013–2014 NHL season.

Hockey is dangerous enough even with the proper gear. Hall of Fame member Pat LaFontaine was forced to retire from hockey after a series of head injuries.

When they joined the NHL in 1972, the Islanders did not always wear helmets. It was not until 1979 that the league made helmets mandatory in order to prevent injuries. Today, the Islanders wear blue and white protective helmets with the team's logo printed on both sides and each player's jersey number on the back. The helmets also include a clear visor attached to help protect players' eyes.

Many goaltenders are creative with their helmets and face masks, and have personalized their protective head gear with different colors, characters, and messages. Billy Smith played with the Islanders from 1972 to 1989, and he painted his mask orange, white, and navy blue. The bottom of his mask included the team's name in white.

In recent years, goalie masks have become more and more vibrant. The designs often represent the actual player and not just the team.

The Coaches

Al Arbour coached the Isles for a total of 1,500 games. He finished his Islanders coaching career with 740 wins, 537 losses, and 223 ties.

3 The Isles missed the playoffs in three of the first four seasons under head coach Jack Capuano.

The Islanders have had a total of 15 coaches in their 42 seasons. Of the 15 coaches, only five managed to lead the team to the playoffs. However, of the five coaches who directed the team to the playoffs, three of them stayed for fewer than five seasons. Al Arbour was one of two exceptions. He took the team to the playoffs 15 times and won four Stanley Cups.

AL ARBOUR Al Arbour became the Islanders' coach during the franchise's second season in the NHL. Under his guidance, the team became a consistent playoff force just a few years later. Arbour is currently second among all coaches in NHL history, with nearly 800 wins. He was the coach of all four Islander Stanley Cup Championship teams and was honored with the Jack Adams Award for coach of the year in 1979.

PETER LAVIOLETTE Peter Laviolette took his first head coaching position with the Islanders in 2001. Before he joined the Islanders, they had been in a drought and had not made a playoff appearance in seven years. Though Laviolette only coached the team for two seasons, they made it to the playoffs both times.

JACK CAPUANO Jack Capuano joined the Islanders as an assistant coach in 2005. It was not until 2011 that he was named head coach. In 2013, during Capuano's second full season with the team, he took the Islanders to the playoffs. This was the team's sole playoff appearance during his first four years as coach.

Fans and the Internet

Although the Islanders have not won a championship in 31 seasons, their fans still believe the team can make another run at the Cup.

Since the Islanders joined the NHL in 1972, their fans have had to adapt to new ways to stay connected with the team. In the past, news about the games was spread through the radio, the newspaper, or by word of mouth. Today, the Isles have several different ways for fans to stay informed about the team.

On its home website, the team has a page devoted to all things Islanders on social media. Fans can click on a number of icons, from Facebook to Twitter. The website also connects fans to a blog called Skates on a Plane, written by the team's communications manager. The blog offers pictures and updates about the team.

Signs
of a fan

#1 Islanders fans join the team in growing beards during the playoffs, a tradition started by the team in the 1980s.

#2 Members of the Islanders Kid Zone Club receive discounts to Isles games, T-shirts, membership cards, and email updates about the team.

Legends of the Past

Many great players have suited up for the Isles. A few of them have become icons of the team and the city it represents.

Position: Right Wing
NHL Seasons: 10 (1977–1987)
Born: January 22, 1957, in Montreal, Quebec, Canada

Denis Potvin

Four-time Stanley Cup winner Denis Potvin played with the Islanders for all of his 15-year career. In the 1978–1979 season, he recorded a career-high 70 **assists** and 101 total points. For four seasons in a row, Potvin notched more assists and points than any other player on the team. He won the James Norris Memorial Trophy in 1976, 1978, and 1979 as the best defenseman. He also won the Calder Memorial Trophy in 1974. He joined teammate Mike Bossy in the NHL Hall of Fame in 1991.

Position: Defenseman
NHL Seasons: 15 (1973–1988)
Born: October 29, 1953, in Ottawa, Ontario, Canada

Mike Bossy

Mike Bossy played with the Islanders for his entire NHL career. During that time, he was the team's leading goal scorer for nine straight seasons, scoring more than 50 goals per season. Bossy won four Stanley Cups and added a long list of personal honors to go with the team's trophies. His achievements include the Calder Memorial Trophy for **rookie** of the year in 1978, and the Conn Smythe Trophy for most valuable player (MVP) of the playoffs in 1982. Bossy also took home the Lady Byng Memorial Trophy for sportsmanship in 1983, 1984, and 1986. He was inducted into the NHL Hall of Fame in 1991.

Bryan Trottier

In his first five seasons with the Islanders, Bryan Trottier was awarded four trophies. He won the Calder Memorial Trophy in 1976, the Hart Memorial Trophy in 1979, the Art Ross Trophy in 1979, and the Conn Smythe Trophy in 1980. He is the only Islander to have ever won the Hart and Ross trophies, which recognized him as the league's MVP and the league's leader in points, respectively. Trottier was inducted into the NHL Hall of Fame in 1997.

Position: Center
NHL Seasons: 18 (1975–1994)
Born: July 17, 1956, in Val Marie, Saskatchewan, Canada

Billy Smith

After playing with the Los Angeles Kings for one season, Billy Smith joined the Islanders in 1972 and played for the New York team until 1989. During the 1982–1983 season, 1,195 shots were taken against Smith. Luckily, he was able to save most of them, earning a .906 **save percentage**. He won the Vezina Trophy for best goalie in 1982, the Conn Smythe Trophy in 1983, and the William M. Jennings Trophy, another award for best goalie, in 1983. He became a member of the NHL Hall of Fame in 1993.

Position: Goaltender
NHL Seasons: 18 (1971–1989)
Born: December 12, 1950, in Perth, Ontario, Canada

Stars of Today

Today's Isles team is made up of many young, talented players who have proven that they are among the best in the league.

Kyle Okposo

Kyle Okposo joined the Islanders as the seventh overall pick in the 2006 NHL **Entry Draft**. Okposo's first NHL goal against the New Jersey Devils was a game winner, establishing him as a clutch player with a knack for scoring important goals. During his next season with the Islanders, Okposo led the team in goals scored, three of which were game winners. Okposo again led the team in goals during the 2013–2014 season with 27, this time, four of his goals sent the Islanders home as victors.

Position: Right Wing
NHL Seasons: 8 (2007–Present)
Born: April 16, 1988, in St. Paul, Minnesota, United States

Johnny Boychuk

Position: Defenseman
NHL Seasons: 8 (2007–Present)
Born: January 19, 1984, in Edmonton, Alberta, Canada

Late in the 2014 off-season, the New York Islanders received a nice surprise when Johnny Boychuk suddenly became available. He no longer fit within the Boston Bruins' **salary cap structure**. The Islanders pounced and acquired the stellar defenseman in exchange for three draft picks. The addition of the one-time Stanley Cup champion immediately strengthened the Islanders' back **line**. The Islanders also hope that Boychuk's winning ways and six years of experience will rub off on their youngsters as the team pursues the same sort of sustained success that Boychuk's Bruins enjoyed during his time in Boston.

John Tavares

During his first year with the Islanders, John Tavares recorded a team-high 54 points. For the next three seasons, Tavares continued to power the Islanders' offense, leading the team in total points. He also led the team in assists for two straight seasons. In his rookie season with the Islanders, he was selected as a member of the NHL All-Rookie Team. In 2012, he played in his first **All-Star** game. Tavares was named team captain prior to the 2013 season.

Position: Center
NHL Seasons: 6 (2009–Present)
Born: September 20, 1990, in Mississauga, Ontario, Canada

All-Time Records

69
Most Goals in a Single Season
During the 1978–1979 season, Mike Bossy scored 69 goals. His franchise record remains unchallenged.

19
Most Playoff Series Victories in a Row
Among their 22 playoff appearances, the Islanders won 19 series in a row, a record that has yet to be matched by any other NHL team.

853
Most Career Assists
NHL Hall of Fame member Bryan Trottier leads all Islanders in career assists, with 853.

8,044
Most Career Saves

Goalie Rick DiPietro played with the Islanders from 2001 to 2013. During that time, he made more saves, 8,044, than any other Islanders goalie.

54
Most Wins in a Single Season

During the 1981–1982 season, the Islanders managed to win a franchise-record 54 games.

Timeline

Throughout the team's history, the New York Islanders have had many memorable events that have become defining moments for the team and its fans.

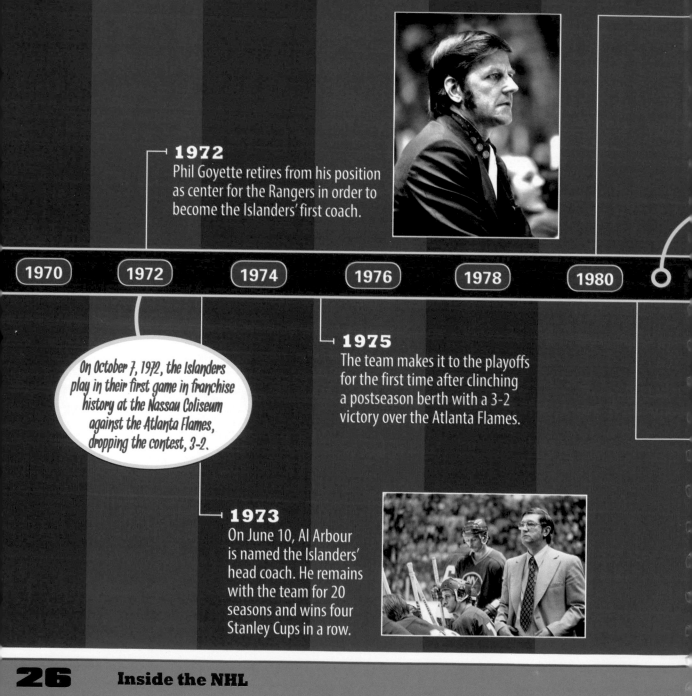

1972
Phil Goyette retires from his position as center for the Rangers in order to become the Islanders' first coach.

1970   1972   1974   1976   1978   1980

On October 7, 1972, the Islanders play in their first game in franchise history at the Nassau Coliseum against the Atlanta Flames, dropping the contest, 3-2.

1975
The team makes it to the playoffs for the first time after clinching a postseason berth with a 3-2 victory over the Atlanta Flames.

1973
On June 10, Al Arbour is named the Islanders' head coach. He remains with the team for 20 seasons and wins four Stanley Cups in a row.

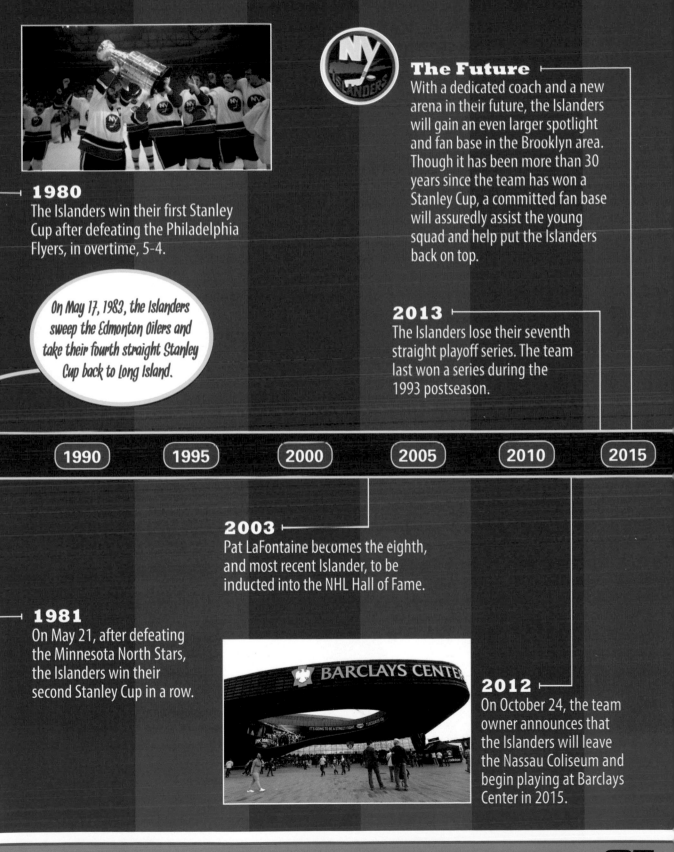

1980
The Islanders win their first Stanley Cup after defeating the Philadelphia Flyers, in overtime, 5-4.

On May 17, 1983, the Islanders sweep the Edmonton Oilers and take their fourth straight Stanley Cup back to Long Island.

The Future
With a dedicated coach and a new arena in their future, the Islanders will gain an even larger spotlight and fan base in the Brooklyn area. Though it has been more than 30 years since the team has won a Stanley Cup, a committed fan base will assuredly assist the young squad and help put the Islanders back on top.

2013
The Islanders lose their seventh straight playoff series. The team last won a series during the 1993 postseason.

1990 1995 2000 2005 2010 2015

2003
Pat LaFontaine becomes the eighth, and most recent Islander, to be inducted into the NHL Hall of Fame.

1981
On May 21, after defeating the Minnesota North Stars, the Islanders win their second Stanley Cup in a row.

BARCLAYS CENTER

2012
On October 24, the team owner announces that the Islanders will leave the Nassau Coliseum and begin playing at Barclays Center in 2015.

Write a Biography

Life Story

A person's life story can be the subject of a book. This kind of book is called a biography. Biographies often describe the lives of people who have achieved great success. These people may be alive today, or they may have lived many years ago. Reading a biography can help you learn more about a great person.

Get the Facts

Use this book, and research in the library and on the internet, to find out more about your favorite Islander. Learn as much about this player as you can. What position does he play? What are his statistics in important categories? Has he set any records? Also, be sure to write down key events in the person's life. What was his childhood like? What has he accomplished off the field? Is there anything else that makes this person special or unusual?

Use the Concept Web

A concept web is a useful research tool. Read the questions in the concept web on the following page. Answer the questions in your notebook. Your answers will help you write a biography.

Concept Web

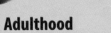

Adulthood
- Where does this individual currently reside?
- Does he or she have a family?

Your Opinion
- What did you learn from the books you read in your research?
- Would you suggest these books to others?
- Was anything missing from these books?

Childhood
- Where and when was this person born?
- Describe his or her parents, siblings, and friends.
- Did this person grow up in unusual circumstances?

Accomplishments off the Field
- What is this person's life's work?
- Has he or she received awards or recognition for accomplishments?
- How have this person's accomplishments served others?

Write a Biography

Help and Obstacles
- Did this individual have a positive attitude?
- Did he or she receive help from others?
- Did this person have a mentor?
- Did this person face any hardships?
- If so, how were the hardships overcome?

Accomplishments on the Field
- What records does this person hold?
- What key games and plays have defined his career?
- What are his stats in categories important to his position?

Work and Preparation
- What was this person's education?
- What was his or her work experience?
- How does this person work?
- What is the process he or she uses?

Trivia Time

Take this quiz to test your knowledge of the Islanders. The answers are printed upside down under each question.

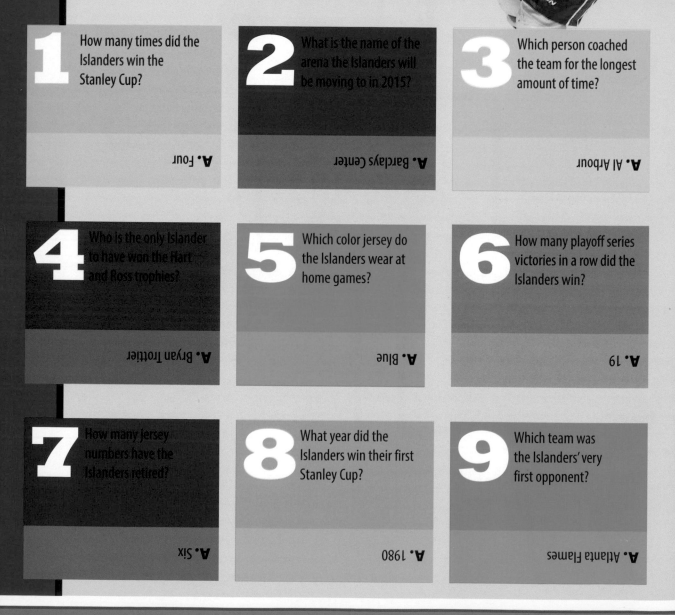

1 How many times did the Islanders win the Stanley Cup?

A. Four

2 What is the name of the arena the Islanders will be moving to in 2015?

A. Barclays Center

3 Which person coached the team for the longest amount of time?

A. Al Arbour

4 Who is the only Islander to have won the Hart and Ross trophies?

A. Bryan Trottier

5 Which color jersey do the Islanders wear at home games?

A. Blue

6 How many playoff series victories in a row did the Islanders win?

A. 19

7 How many jersey numbers have the Islanders retired?

A. Six

8 What year did the Islanders win their first Stanley Cup?

A. 1980

9 Which team was the Islanders' very first opponent?

A. Atlanta Flames

Key Words

All-Star: a game made for the best-ranked players in the NHL that happens mid-season. A player can be named an All-Star and then be sent to play in this game.

assists: a statistic that is attributed to up to two players of the scoring team who shoot, pass, or deflect the puck toward the scoring teammate

entry draft: an annual meeting where different teams in the NHL are allowed to pick new, young players who can join their teams

franchise: a team that is a member of a professional sports league

line: forwards who play in a group, or "shift," during a game

logo: a symbol that stands for a team or organization

playoffs: a series of games that occur after regular season play

rookie: a player age 26 or younger who has played no more than 25 games in a previous season, nor six or more games in two previous seasons

salary cap structure: the total amount of money that the NHL owners are allowed to pay their players. It is a "hard" cap, meaning there are no exceptions. The latest salary cap sits at $69 million per team.

save percentage: the rate at which a goalie stops shots being made toward his net by the opposing team

territorial fee: each NHL team owns a territorial right to its home city and surrounding geographical region. The extent and distance of these territorial rights differs widely from team to team. When one team attempts to occupy the territory of another franchise, it must be willing to pay a hefty territorial fee to the home team.

Index

Log on to www.av2books.com

AV² by Weigl brings you media enhanced books that support active learning. Go to www.av2books.com, and enter the special code found on page 2 of this book. You will gain access to enriched and enhanced content that supplements and complements this book. Content includes video, audio, weblinks, quizzes, a slide show, and activities.

AV² Online Navigation

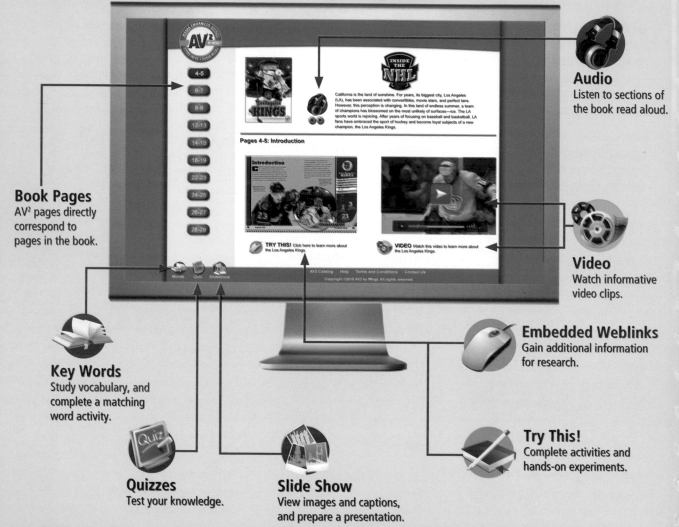

Audio
Listen to sections of the book read aloud.

Book Pages
AV² pages directly correspond to pages in the book.

Video
Watch informative video clips.

Key Words
Study vocabulary, and complete a matching word activity.

Embedded Weblinks
Gain additional information for research.

Quizzes
Test your knowledge.

Slide Show
View images and captions, and prepare a presentation.

Try This!
Complete activities and hands-on experiments.

AV² was built to bridge the gap between print and digital. We encourage you to tell us what you like and what you want to see in the future.

Sign up to be an AV² Ambassador at www.av2books.com/ambassador.